DOG OWNER'S GUIDE TO THE
Boxer

Andrew Brace

FIREFLY BOOKS

A FIREFLY BOOK

Published by Firefly Books Ltd. 2005

Copyright © 2005 Ringpress Books Limited

First printing

Publisher Cataloging-in-Publication Data (U.S.)

Brace, Andrew.
  Boxer/Andrew Brace.
[80] p. : col. photos. ; cm.
(Dog owner's guide)
Summary: A dog owner's guide to the care and training of boxers.
ISBN 1-55407-073-2
1. Boxer (dog breed). I. Title. II. Series.
636.73 22 SF429.B75M35 2005

Library and Archives Canada Cataloguing in Publication

Brace, Andrew H
  Boxer/Andrew Brace.
(Dog owner's guide)
ISBN 1-55407-073-2
1. Boxer (Dog breed) I. Title.
II. Series.
SF429.B75B73 2005 636.73
C2005-900982-9

Published in the United States by
Firefly Books (U.S.) Inc.
P.O. Box 1338, Ellicott Station
Buffalo, New York 14205

Published in Canada by
Firefly Books Ltd.
66 Leek Crescent
Richmond Hill, Ontario L4B 1H1

Printed in China

This book is dedicated to the memory of Bruce, a Boxer, who was my first pedigree dog. Although Bruce never saw the inside of a show ring, he kindled in me a fascination and passion for the world of show dogs and dog shows that has never waned. My best friend through those difficult teenage years, Bruce, died tragically young, but he will always have a special place in my heart.

CONTENTS

1

HISTORY OF THE BOXER

The modern Boxer owes his early origins to the combination of a German hunting and baiting breed, known as the Bullenbeisser, and the primitive English Bulldog.

However, a much more charming account comes in the shape of a legend that has been passed down among German peasants for generations. This is quoted in Herr Philip Stockmann's book on the breed.

THE BOXER LEGEND

"In the beginning was creation, and on the sixth day, after the world and the heavens were made, God created the animals to inhabit it, in every possible variety for every possible purpose; and he created Man to have dominion over the animal. But so that Man should not be alone among the animals, he made one animal to be Man's friend—the dog.

"And He made the dogs in many different forms so that every man could choose his favorite companion—large and small, tall and short, brown, black, white, spotted and striped, shaggy and smooth. And God saw that they were good. So good that He said 'I will make one dog who is supreme, one above all other dogs, who shall have beauty, strength, speed and courage, blended subtly with loyalty, nobility, watchfulness and friendliness.'

"So He took soft clay and from it fashioned the ideal dog, in the shape of a Boxer, except that, like other dogs, he had a long, sensitive, elegant nose, the very acme of noses. As he put it aside to harden, God was pleased, and said 'Truly this is the perfect dog.'

"Now although the Boxer had not hardened, he was in all other respects complete, and he heard what God said about him, which made him very proud. Therefore, as he went his way, he said to the other dogs 'I am the perfect dog, because I heard God say so. Look at me and you must admit that I am a better dog than you.'

"The little dogs agreed at once; the medium dogs were not so sure but were not prepared to dispute

the point; but the larger dogs were decidedly annoyed, for were they not bigger and stronger than the Boxer? They said as much, taunting the Boxer for his size, until, in a rage, the Boxer hurled himself upon the largest.

"But alas! He had forgotten that he was still soft, and his beautiful nose, the symmetrical perfection of all noses, was squashed flat, his smooth face was all wrinkled, and when he saw this he was very worried.

"Then God, who had seen all that had taken place, smiled, and said 'Because you are my favorite, you shall have only the punishment you have made for yourself. For all time you must wear your face as you have made it this day.'

"That this is true cannot be doubted, because to this day, the Boxer meets all small dogs with courtesy and will not harm them; but he has not forgiven the large dogs, and if provoked, will still hurl himself upon them in rage."

Anyone who has shared their life with a Boxer will fully understand that he was God's favorite, and the many endearing attributes of the breed mentioned in this delightful piece of folklore persist to this day.

THE FIRST BOXERS

Towards the end of the 19th century, George Alt, a resident of Munich, Germany, produced a bitch who was called Alt's Schecken.

Previously, Alt had mated Flora, a brindle-colored bitch of medium Bullenbeisser type, which he had imported from France, to a local dog of unknown ancestry, but known simply as "Boxer."

The union resulted in a fawn-

The Boxer: According to folklore, he was chosen as God's favorite.

Breed pioneers set out to create the ideal dog in looks and temperament.

However it was Flocki's sister, Ch. Blanka von Angertor, a white bitch, who was to be of greater influence. When Blanka was mated to Piccolo von Angertor (a grandson of Lechner's Boxer, Blanka's grandsire), she produced a predominantly white bitch called Meta von der Passage, who is still considered to be the mother of the breed.

and-white male, this dog taking his owner's name, to become simply "Lechner's Boxer." He was, in turn, mated back to his own dam, Flora, and one of their offspring was Schecken.

Schecken was later mated to an English Bulldog called Tom, who produced the historically significant dog called Flocki.

Early photographs of Meta show her to be rather long and weak-backed, less than straight-fronted, and quite down-faced.

Yet, through her progeny, she provided a foundation for the future of the breed to which, now, she bears little resemblance.

Flocki earned his place in Boxer history by becoming the very first Boxer to enter the German Stud Book. He did so by winning at a Munich show for St. Bernards; the first event to schedule a class for Boxers.

9

THE FIRST BREED CLUB

In 1896, the German Boxer Club was formed and, in March of that year, the club held its first show, which attracted 20 entries for the judge, Elard Konig.

We are told that several of the entered dogs were white, or white with patches of either brindle or fawn, while others were black.

Following its first show, the parent club set about establishing a Standard for the Boxer, which was eventually adopted in January 1902.

Breed Pioneers

Some seven years later, in 1909, a young German lady who was studying art and sculpture in Munich, met up with a young man who proved to be a Boxer owner.

The lady, named Friederun, first became enchanted with the Boxer breed when she saw a photograph in a book of dog breeds given to her for Christmas by her brother. She longed for a Boxer from that day forward and, having discovered that

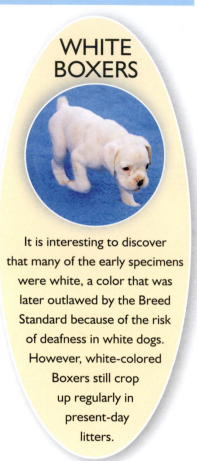

WHITE BOXERS

It is interesting to discover that many of the early specimens were white, a color that was later outlawed by the Breed Standard because of the risk of deafness in white dogs. However, white-colored Boxers still crop up regularly in present-day litters.

Philip Stockmann owned such a dog, she encouraged their friendship and subsequently they married.

Herr Stockmann's dog, Pluto, became his bride's most devoted

companion and awakened in her the desire to learn more about the breed.

Frau Stockmann's contribution to the breed can never be overestimated. In subsequent years, she and her husband established the legendary Kennel von Dom, which produced some of the most famous and significant dogs in the breed's history. In her book, *My Life With Boxers*, she relates her most fascinating life story, and tells of the hardship and the heartaches she faced— and the moments of joy—while struggling to keep her kennel alive through the war years.

In later years, the German, Dutch, British and American Boxers may have evolved along slightly different lines, but there can be no disputing the fact that all owe their foundation to Frau Stockmann and her von Doms.

The influence of key dogs such as Sigurd von Dom, his son Zorm von Dom, and grandsons Utz and Lustig von Dom, was vast on both sides of the Atlantic.

The Boxer is a popular show dog throughout the world.

11

THE BREED

Every pedigree dog has a Breed Standard, a written blueprint for the breed. This "word picture" describes what the ideal Boxer should look like, what his temperament should be and how he should move. The essential points for the Boxer breed are as follows:

GENERAL APPEARANCE

The Boxer is a noble dog, squarely built, with strong bone and great musculation.

TEMPERAMENT

A typical Boxer is fearless, yet biddable. He should always appear self-assured.

HEAD

The Boxer head is unique and, in the show ring, a good head is of outstanding importance. The head should be in proportion to

The Breed Standard is a blueprint for the ideal Boxer.

STANDARD OF THE BOXER

STOP

OCCIPUT

WITHERS

TOPLINE

CROUP

MUZZLE

CHEST

TUCK UP

STIFLE

HOCK

PASTERN

the rest of the body. The skull should be clean and lean; the muzzle is broad and deep. The lower jaw is slightly undershot, and curves slightly upward.

EYES

Dark brown in color, and forward looking. The eyes should convey an impression of intelligence and character.

EARS

In the U.S., and some European countries, the ears are cropped. The result is that the ears stand upright, enhancing the alert expression of the dog.

Natural ears are set well apart on the widest point of the skull, and they lie close to the cheek when the Boxer is relaxed. They fall forward, with a distinct crease when the dog is alert.

MOUTH

The Boxer is one of the few breeds where the teeth meet in an undershot bite, meaning the lower incisors protrude slightly beyond the upper.

NECK

Strong and muscular, with an elegant arch to the withers (the high point of the shoulders).

FOREQUARTERS

Long and sloping shoulders; straight, parallel forelegs, of good bone.

BODY

The Boxer should present a square profile with a deep chest, reaching to the elbows. The back should be broad and strongly muscled.

Great importance is placed on the correct head proportions.

It should be short and straight, with a slight downwards slope towards the tail.

HINDQUARTERS
Strong and muscular, with long, broad thighs. The underline should show a gradual tuck-up.

PAWS
Small and catlike, with arched toes and hard pads.

TAIL
The breed was developed with a docked tail, but legislation now outlaws this in many countries.

MOVEMENT
Strong and powerful with great reach in front, and powerful drive from behind.

COAT
Fawn or brindle with white markings. The fawn can range from pale to a deep, deer-red. The brindle markings should stand out clearly on a fawn background.

SIZE
Males: 22.5–25 inches (57–63 cm) at the shoulder. Females: 21–23 inches (53–59 cm).

In the United States and Canada the ears are cropped, giving a most distinctive look.

DIVERSITY OF TYPE

One of the major bones of contention in recent years has been the diversity of type within the breed.

Broadly speaking, European dogs have evolved as a stockier type, with great emphasis being placed on head and mouth points, and perhaps more importance accorded to the forequarters than the hindquarters.

North Americans have favored a more upstanding and stylish Boxer, with a cleaner head and slightly longer muzzle.

Meanwhile, British dogs, thanks to a wide variety of imports from both the United States and Europe, have tended to produce a more middle-of-the-road type of Boxer, which can frequently find favor with visiting judges.

Type may vary from country to country, but the Boxer remains true to the original ideal.

2

CHOOSING A BOXER

The fact that you have bought this book suggests that you have decided that the Boxer is the breed for you. But is it?

Only the most irresponsible of breeders will try to sell a puppy to a potentially unsuitable owner, so the chances are that you will be questioned (in some cases interrogated!) by the breeder you contact, as regards the likelihood of your making a responsible Boxer owner.

So, before you go in pursuit of your puppy, you must be positive that this is the breed for you.

BREED CHARACTERISTICS

To begin with, let us look at the Boxer's sheer size. He is a medium to large breed, weighing anything between 55–70 pounds (25–32 kg), depending on the sex, and measuring between 21–25 inches (53–63 cm) in height, so, although described in the Breed Standard as a medium-sized dog, the Boxer has considerable bulk and strength.

The fact that the breed has a short foreface and well-padded muzzle means that the Boxer's smiling face will invariably conceal a goodly helping of saliva—"slobber" to the uninitiated.

If you are house-proud, think twice before contemplating a Boxer. While essentially clean and quite fastidious in their habits, Boxers think nothing of having a good old shake and sending strings of slobber flying. The fact that they could land on your midnight-blue velvet curtains is to be considered!

TAILPIECE

The general perception of the Boxer is a breed with a short, stumpy tail and a bottom that wags ceaselessly. In some European countries, thanks to new legislation, fewer Boxer puppies are having their tails docked. However, in the United States and Canada tails are still routinely docked.

TEMPERAMENT

The Boxer's temperament should always be beyond reproach. While he has many clownlike qualities and seems blessed with an acute sense of humor and fun, it should always be remembered that he has been bred down from stock that were versatile working and guard dogs. Consequently, a Boxer has a deep-seated instinct to protect his home and family, yet this should in no way make him provocative or quarrelsome.

Brainy Breed

The breed has great intelligence, with a brain that needs to be kept occupied. The Boxer thrives on company—human and canine—and no Boxer will flourish if he is forced to spend long periods of time alone. He will, in the absence of any suitable mental stimulus, resort to making his own entertainment, and that could mean anything from taking down curtains to remodeling the new three-piece suite. Remember what is said about the Devil and

The Boxer is a wonderful family companion.

idle hands; or paws, in this case.

As with any dog, be it pedigree or mongrel, it is inadvisable to think of becoming a puppy owner unless there is likely to be someone at home virtually all day. Very few responsible breeders would consider selling one of

their lovingly reared puppies to a household where two partners are out at work all day.

Boxers are great family dogs and get on well with children, provided those children are taught firmly to respect them and do not abuse them in any way.

Bringing up a child and a puppy together is beneficial to both, and a dog should, in my opinion, be a compulsory part of any childhood, but I suppose I am biased.

This is a breed that requires mental stimulation

EXERCISE NEEDS

Boxers are, like their namesakes, muscular animals and, to keep in shape, they need plenty of exercise of varying kinds. They benefit from both road work and free galloping and, although a vast yard is not essential, they do need some space.

There are always exceptions to the rule, and one of the fittest Boxers I know lives in a small house in a large city. However, he is owned by two of the fittest people I know, and the dog gets exercise at a park at least four times a day.

The size and location of your home is incidental to your

becoming a suitable Boxer owner. Provided your house and yard are totally secure, that you are prepared to exercise your Boxer regularly, come rain or shine, and that he will have company for most of the day, you and your Boxer could become an ideal partnership.

Plan a program of leash-walking and free-running exercise.

TRAINING TARGETS

Puppies do not teach themselves. If you are serious about becoming a Boxer owner, you must be prepared to school both yourself and your dog in basic disciplines. Your Boxer must be taught to come when he is called, to sit on command, and to go to his bed when told. Boxer owners who neglect these vital disciplines early on in their puppies' lives rue the day, as very soon they find themselves with an unruly adolescent who has a very definite will of his own. Sadly, many such cases end up in rescue. Their only crime is having an owner who was too lazy to teach them basic good manners.

CHOOSING AN OLDER DOG

Most potential dog owners automatically think that the only route to dog ownership is through obtaining a puppy of 9 weeks or thereabouts.

But for some people, particularly those who are not in the first flush of youth, it may be a better solution to give a home to an older dog.

There are always Boxers in rescue through no fault of their own, and many of these make wonderful companions.

There are also some breeders who prefer to place dogs they have finished showing or breeding from into "retirement" pet homes. They believe that it is better for a dog who has done sterling work for them to finish his days in the lap of luxury as a pampered pet, rather than to sit it out in a kennel.

Such dogs may be as young as 4 years old and have another decade or so ahead of them so, unless you are adamant that you must have a puppy, why not consider one of these options?

Do not rule out the option of taking on an older dog.

DOG OR BITCH?

Having decided that a Boxer is the dog for you, you now need to establish whether you would prefer a dog or a bitch. There are pros and cons where both are concerned.

Male dogs do not go into heat, but their hormones are active, and a headstrong male with sex on his mind can prove a handful. Neutering the dog is a sensible solution for most pet owners. In most cases, it is advisable to wait until your dog is around 9 months of age before he is castrated, so he has the chance to reach physical maturity.

Bitches usually go into heat twice a year, causing a little mess around the house and the unwanted attraction of stray males.

The male (left) is more independent.

To avoid the inconvenience of a bitch coming into heat, treatments are available to stop it. However, neutering is the best option if you have no plans to breed from your Boxer bitch. There are a number of health benefits associated with spaying. The risk of developing mammary cancer is reduced, and the chance of pyometra (a serious womb infection) is eliminated.

Please do not think of buying a bitch because you have the misguided idea that "she can pay for herself" by having puppies. Breeding dogs is for the dedicated, the knowledgeable and the responsible.

COLOR

Every Boxer owner, past, present or future, has a favorite color. Some owners always choose fawn dogs, others are equally passionate about brindles.

Then there are whites, of course. Generally speaking, white Boxers are put to sleep at birth, because there is the chance that their hearing may be impaired. Yet some people find whites attractive and, if a dog has colored patches and is not albino, there is a strong possibility that the hearing will be in no way dysfunctional.

Occasionally, breeders will rear a patched white puppy if they have a definite pet sale. However, the registration papers may designate the puppy as "non-breeding."

The fawn color varies from a pale, almost yellow, fawn to a rich deer-red. The brindle coat

Fawn: This can vary from yellow to deer-red.

Brindle: The dark stripes should stand out.

pattern consists of a fawn ground color with black stripes banding the entire colored area. Strictly speaking, such stripes should be in distinct relief to the background color, creating a "tiger-striped" effect. In reality, many Boxers are seen, often winning top honors, where brindling is so heavy that the first impression is that of an almost black dog.

The flashy Boxer with white markings finds favor in the show ring.

MARKINGS

The next consideration is regarding a "plain" or "flashy" dog. The Boxer Breed Standard dictates that up to one-third of the ground color may be white but, in many countries, fashion has decreed that the dogs which find favor in the show ring tend to be flashily marked, i.e., with white trim, usually consisting of a white blaze, white flashes on the muzzle, a white collar and "shirt front," and four white socks.

Few exhibitors persevere with solid-colored Boxers (i.e., dogs devoid of any white markings) in the ring, feeling that they are handicapped under the majority of judges.

If you do not plan to show your Boxer, markings are a matter of personal preference.

This is sad, as conformational excellence should always be of greater importance than cosmetic aspects of the Boxer and, importantly, plain bitches will be far less likely to produce white puppies than their flashier sisters.

"Plain" dogs, however, still win in Germany and Central Europe.

As a consequence of the show ring appeal of flashy markings, many breeders immediately discard plain puppies as "pet quality," although, in truth, they may be anatomically superior Boxers to some of their more glamorous siblings.

So, when pet buyers arrive to view a litter, they may be offered only a choice of plain puppies. However, many longtime Boxer owners may well remember owning a black-faced Boxer with little white, born before "flashy" became the vogue.

3

THE RIGHT PUPPY

Hopefully, you and your Boxer are going to share more than a decade of your lives together.

You are going to become great pals and confidants, and your Boxer will become an important part of your family in every way. It therefore makes sense to spend some time making sure that you get the best possible puppy, and that you do everything in your power to avoid any problems.

Firstly, find a responsible breeder. The best way to do this is by contacting your national kennel club and asking for details

of the Boxer Club in your area. Contact the secretary, explain that you are looking for a Boxer, and express an interest in joining the club.

DO YOUR HOMEWORK

Do not rush into buying your Boxer. Ideally, you should attend a few functions at your local Boxer Club, so that you have the chance to meet breeders. Go to a few shows and talk to as many breeders as possible, concentrating on the kennels who are showing the kind of Boxers you admire.

PET OR SHOW?

If you want a pet puppy and have no intention of showing, say so, and remember that when, 12 months on, some well-meaning but self-appointed dog expert spots you walking your dog and says, "You ought to show him!"

It is true that some great Champions have been discovered that way, but they are very, very few and far between. As for the talent-spotter's experience: you will probably discover that it goes no further than being able to tell one breed from another.

There is nothing more infuriating for a breeder than to sell to a pet home a healthy, typical puppy, who may not be of top show quality due to some minor yet unimportant shortcoming, only to discover that the owner has been talked into showing that dog. Then, when the dog has not won and a judge has pointed out his faults, the owner gets irate with the breeder who didn't sell the puppy as a show prospect in the first place.

Remember, the breeder has a reputation to safeguard.

QUIZ SPOT

Before you are even invited to visit the dogs, the responsible breeder will have asked you all sorts of questions. The breeder has to be as sure as possible that you are a bonafide buyer who can give a puppy a loving and secure home for life. If you are frank with them, they will be fair with you.

29

VISITING THE BREEDER

Telephone the breeder of your choice. Make an appointment to see the adult dogs. Keep the appointment and arrive on time. Dog breeders are very busy people and writing off an hour to entertain prospective customers means that other vital chores are delayed.

Ask any questions about the dogs you feel you want answered, and don't worry about making yourself look silly. If you don't know, ask. Your breeder was once a rank novice, buying his first puppy. Asking now could avoid hours of trouble and worry at a later date.

Find out when the breeder expects to have puppies available. Most reputable breeders have waiting lists, and puppies do not come to order. You may have to wait months, but do wait. Far too many puppy buyers lose patience, snap up the first puppy they see advertised (regardless of his origins), and live to regret the day.

If you are told that a puppy may be available from a specific litter, ask to see the dam of the puppies. If possible, ask to see the sire too, though there is every chance that he may not live at the same kennel, as most breeders travel to use the best available

It is important to see the puppies with their mother.

males, even though they might not own them.

If you are keen to buy a puppy from this breeder, and one is available soon, you may be asked to pay a deposit. This not only serves as a gesture of goodwill on your part, it tends to sort out the time-wasters who so often plague breeders.

RESISTING TEMPTATION

In due course, you get that long-awaited telephone call. You will have told the breeder of your preference as regards sex and color. It is quite possible that a puppy is available, but he is not the sex or color that you have set your heart on.

You will be asked to come to see the puppies anyhow. Think long and hard about this. Are you prepared to take a dog when you really want a bitch, or a brindle though you only like fawns? If you are not happy about taking an alternative, tell the breeder there and then that you would prefer to wait until he or she has another litter. Do not go to see the available puppies. Why? Because you will come home with one, believe me! You will not be able to resist that face in the puppy pen, the black-faced brindle dog who looks up at you so longingly, with head on one side, almost knowing that you really wanted a flashy fawn bitch. It is true that there are often "love matches" such as this, and the partnership remains a lifelong joy, but it is also possible that you could later resent being emotionally blackmailed into taking something you didn't actually want.

ASSESSING THE PUPPIES

When you arrive to see the puppies, ask politely if you can see the whole litter together. Stress that you realize that they are not all for sale, but explain that you would like to see them as a family, so to speak. This way, you will get a good idea of the puppies in a relative sense.

If the breeder sits you down in the kitchen, disappears to the kennel or nursery, then returns to thrust a single puppy into your lap, it is impossible for you to know whether this puppy is half the size of his siblings or much more introverted than they are.

Hopefully, the breeder will be happy to oblige and show you the puppies in their playing area. Look for the following signs of good rearing:

Do not let your heart rule your head when choosing a puppy.

- The puppies should be in a clean, warm, comfortable, fresh-smelling environment.
- The puppies should look well fed and rounded (not potbellied, but pleasantly fat and chunky).
- The pups should appear happy and outgoing.

Before you start falling in love with any puppy, find out which puppies are available to you and forget the rest immediately.

Another golden rule: if you see a puppy who appears timid and tries to run away when the others rush forward with eager anticipation, do not feel sorry for him and long to take him home and love him. This puppy may well have a temperament problem, which will, should you choose to buy him, cause untold heartache in years to come.

Temperament

You want a bruiser of a puppy who is not afraid of anything; this is the sort of temperament you can channel and build on. Nervousness is not something you want to have to cope with.

Having been shown which puppies are available, concentrate on them and ask to see them apart from the unavailable puppies. Looking at the others will only cloud the issue.

The breeder should be happy for you to handle the puppies, provided you have met with any requirements they may insist upon as regards disinfecting.

As well as being outgoing and well covered with flesh, a well-reared puppy should have a clear coat. Run your hand against the grain of the coat to check for fleas, scurf or any other skin

The puppies in the litter should be bold, lively and confident.

problem. Check that the ears are clean and not foul-smelling or clogged with wax.

Play with the puppies and see if one "chooses" you. If there is such a puppy, this is the one to take home. Dogs have wonderful instincts and are very quick to latch on to a character with whom they will be compatible. When a Boxer puppy chooses you, you will be his for life.

PICKING OUT A SHOW PROSPECT

If you are looking for a show prospect, there are a number of specialized technicalities to bear in mind, and there are much more detailed publications available for such buyers. However, here are a few tips worth remembering.

When the puppy runs around, he should move freely and without effort, with a look of power, showing a firm, strong back and proud neck. People who are not used to seeing large numbers of very young Boxer puppies are sometimes concerned that they appear to have rather pointed heads. A very pronounced occiput is simply an indication of a very well-balanced head in adulthood, and not the result of an accident.

The breeder will help you to assess show potential.

COLLECTING YOUR PUPPY

Take a blanket and an old cardboard box with you when you collect your puppy. Place it on the back seat of the car, puppy inside, with someone sitting alongside to offer reassurance.

This is probably your puppy's first car journey, so be prepared for him to be sick. Do not worry: it is a natural reaction. However, you are advised to be prepared and take some paper towels to clean up with.

Most breeders will give you a supply of food to last a day or two, so that you avoid any drastic changes and risk an upset stomach.

At last the big day arrives when it is time to collect your puppy.

ARRIVING HOME

When you get home, put your puppy straight into the yard where he may wish to relieve himself; if he has not already done so in the car. Give him time to acclimatize himself to the surroundings, sniffing around and exploring. Do not rush him and do not invite the neighbors around for a viewing session. Leaving home will be enough of a trauma for the puppy for one day.

Show your puppy his bed, and make sure that is the place where he always sleeps.

SLEEPING QUARTERS

You should have sorted out where your puppy is going to sleep (for the rest of his life) and that is where he should sleep from day one.

Do not weaken when he cries at night and smuggle him upstairs to the bedroom. If you do, you will be sorry!

Every dog should have his own space, a place that is his and his alone, away from the general hubbub of the household, the kids and the television. This should be his retreat, his refuge.

GREAT CRATES

I am a great advocate of the dog crate. My advice is to invest in one that is large enough to house a fully-grown Boxer when standing up. The ideal type is made of heavy-duty metal mesh, with a hinged and lockable door to the front. They are not cheap, but they are a once-in-a-lifetime purchase and will prove invaluable.

CRATE-TRAINING

The crate should be situated in the place that is to be your Boxer's own area, ideally in a kitchen corner or utility area. The position should be warm and draft-free. The crate should be lined with newspaper in case of accidents.

Place a heavy-duty cardboard box in the crate, with the front cut out to facilitate easy access. Put some old blankets and chewable but indestructible toys in the box, and leave your puppy in the box, crate locked, for ten minutes or so.

He will cry and protest, but talk to him reassuringly and soothingly, without any physical contact. He will soon realize that you are not going to leave him, you are pleased with him and, after he has done a ten-minute "stretch," open the door, let him greet you, and you can cuddle him to your heart's content.

At bedtime, put the pup in his crate and leave him there for the night, without any contact whatsoever, no matter how much he objects. Giving in to his pathetic whining at this early stage will only be storing up trouble for later.

A puppy must learn to spend some time on his own.

4 CARING FOR YOUR BOXER

The Boxer is a relatively easily maintained breed, requiring moderate exercise, a well-balanced diet, little by way of grooming, kind discipline and lots of tender loving care.

Get to know your Boxer as an individual, finding out the most suitable diet, planning an exercise program, and keeping up to date with preventive health care.

FEEDING

Your puppy's breeder should have given you a diet sheet, and this should not only include the meals at the age when you collect him, but right through into adulthood. Try to adhere to the diet sheet as closely as possible, but if, having read it, you feel that the recommended diet will not suit

your lifestyle, discuss it with the breeder. Feeding dogs is no great mystery. Provided your Boxer receives a balanced diet, it will be easy for you to hit on a feeding regime that suits you both.

Not that many years ago, the majority of breeders fed what was basically a meat-and-kibble

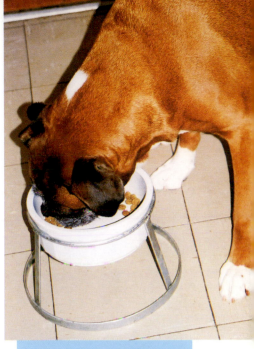

combination. This did not satisfy all a dog's nutritional needs and, consequently, the basic diet was supplemented by calcium compounds during the growing stages, and various other additives thereafter.

These days, highly qualified canine dieticians have taken the guesswork out of feeding. They have formulated a myriad of complex diets that contain all the necessary additives a dog needs at any given time of his life. They produce not only one complete feed, but a whole range within one product label.

You will find today that most "completes" have at least three grades of feeds: one for growth (suitable for puppies and youngsters who have yet to reach

Canine nutritionists have taken the guesswork out of feeding.

full maturity), one for high activity (for adult dogs who lead active lives), and one for less activity (for older dogs who use less energy).

FOLLOW INSTRUCTIONS

If you feed a commercial brand, it is vitally important that you follow the manufacturer's instructions religiously. If the food is complete, it should need no additives, as long as you are feeding the correct amount. Many puppies are ruined by overenthusiastic owners who cannot resist the latest miracle "supplement," brightly packaged on the pet store shelf.

Make sure fresh drinking water is always available.

MILK OR WATER?

Many pet owners have the misguided belief that puppies have to be given cow's or goat's milk. But once they have finished with their mother's milk, water should be all the fluid they need.

As soon as your puppy arrives home, he should have a heavy, nonspill water dish, which should be checked regularly for a supply of clean, fresh water. This is doubly important if you are feeding a dry complete food.

MEALTIMES

The number of meals given per day should again be detailed in your Boxer puppy's diet sheet. Most puppies leave home when they are on about four meals per day and, eventually, by the time they are 18 months old, they should be able to suffice with one meal a day.

Many pet owners feel guilty about leaving their Boxers 24 hours between meals, and so prefer to give a light breakfast and a slightly reduced main meal later in the day. You should choose what suits you best, and stick to it. Dogs are very much creatures of habit and do not appreciate their feeding routine being upset.

I currently have one elderly dog by whom you can set your watch: at 5 p.m. each day, on the dot, she is standing over her feeding bowl in anticipation, and woe betide me if I am so much as five minutes late!

From the very start, you should decide where you are going to feed your Boxer and ignore his pleading face at your own dinner table. Any attempt to jump up at the table must be swiftly corrected and the dog pushed into a sitting position; never reward such behavior with a tasty morsel from your plate.

Better still, when the human members of your family sit down to eat, give your Boxer the "Crate" command. In this way, he will soon learn that the family dinner table is no concern of his and he will be happy to take a nap at your mealtimes.

THE CASE FOR BONES

Your Boxer puppy will appreciate a cooked marrowbone to gnaw on; particularly when he is teething. Make sure you avoid smaller bones that can splinter or be accidentally swallowed. Personally, I am reluctant to give cow hooves or rawhide chews at this stage, as there is a danger of the puppy swallowing bits that are too big for him to cope with. Dogs should always be supervised when they are given bones or any type of chew.

DEWORMING

When you collect your puppy, the breeder should have given you full details of the pup's deworming treatment to date.

Puppies should be dewormed for roundworms, before and after they leave the breeder. Tapeworms, whipworms and hookworms are also common problems that need to be treated.

Heartworm, spread by mosquitoes, can be fatal to dogs, and is endemic to parts of the Unites States and Canada. An annual test for heartworm is important, followed by seasonal preventive treatment.

Give your puppy a day or two to settle in, and then take him to your local vet for a complete checkup. On this first visit, show the vet details of any dewormings and ask for the suggested subsequent treatments. Be sure to carry your puppy into the waiting room and do not put him on the floor. He is still very vulnerable to disease, so be

Deworming should be carried out on a routine basis.

vigilant in this respect.

Some deworming treatments will dissolve worms before they are expelled, but some worms will be passed. It is advisable to check stools as you carry out your daily cleanup.

VACCINATIONS

Puppies are routinely vaccinated against distemper, hepatitis, parvovirus and parainfluenza. Vaccinating against leptospurosis is also recommended in areas where the disease is endemic. Vaccination against rabies is compulsory in Canada and parts of the United States. Your vet will advise you on when these shots should be given.

You will receive a vaccination certificate, which should be kept in a safe place. In fact, it is as well to keep all your Boxer's paperwork in the same place as other important family documents. All too easily, they can get stuffed in the back of a drawer and can never be found when they may be required, sometimes urgently.

Your vet will notify you when your Boxer requires a booster shot and, on those visits, most vets will automatically give such patients a routine thorough checkup, any major health problems will be spotted at this time.

The timing of vaccinations may vary, depending on where you live.

FOLLOW INSTRUCTIONS

If you plan putting your Boxer into a boarding kennel at some stage, you may need a vaccination against kennel cough in addition to the standard shots. This will also be recorded on your dog's vaccination certificate, and the boarding kennel owner will ask to see this when you check your dog in. Without it, few kennels will accept a boarder.

HOUSING

I have already stressed the value of training your Boxer to sleep in a crate, and getting him used to being put in the crate whenever you feel it is necessary. This assumes that your Boxer is going to be essentially a house dog, as opposed to a kennel dog.

No dog thrives in a kennel alone, and I cannot recommend investing in a kennel and run if you own just one Boxer. Two dogs together, however, are a different matter and they will enjoy their time, free of humans.

They will, nonetheless, appreciate their time spent in the house with the family.

A kennel and run is fine if you have more than one Boxer.

EXERCISE

Playing in the yard is sufficient exercise for a growing pup.

Many Boxer owners make the fatal mistake of thinking that their growing puppy needs vast amounts of exercise to help him grow big and strong. In truth, those growing bones are actually quite delicate and, for the first six months of his life, your Boxer puppy's exercise should be restricted to playing in your yard.

During this time, he can become accustomed to his leash and collar, and you can begin basic training (see Chapter 5).

If you do not have a large enough yard, then small, gentle walks to the park will suffice. Long, sustained walks and galloping sessions should only be started after six months, and then introduced very gradually if you are not to do more harm than good.

GROOMING

The Boxer is one of the easiest breeds to groom, with his short, close and shining coat. It is a good idea to get your Boxer puppy used to being handled in a weekly maintenance check. Not only will this assure you that he is clean and healthy, but it will prepare him for future close inspections by veterinarians or—who knows?—by dog show judges.

Teeth

Make your puppy show you his teeth, and do not take "No" for an answer. Start this routine when your puppy is small and he has no choice in the matter. After all; you are the boss. Vets can get a little impatient with boisterous adult Boxers who have never been taught to have their mouths opened, and tempers can run high.

Plenty of chewing on big marrowbones should help keep your Boxer's teeth clean and free of tartar; this is particularly important if you are feeding a complete diet where no real grinding is called for.

From a very early age, get your Boxer used to having his teeth cleaned with proprietary dog

Accustom your puppy to having his teeth examined.

toothpaste. This should be applied with a harsh toothbrush, but be careful not to make the gums bleed in your enthusiasm.

Eyes

Your Boxer's eyes should sparkle with health, and the only area to watch here is the inner corners from which may come a slight tearstain. A weekly swab with lukewarm water and cotton wool should keep this in check.

Make sure that any folds of skin around the muzzle are always dried thoroughly after bathing. Severe staining can be treated with proprietary products which have been specially designed for the purpose.

Ears

Ears should be inspected, and they should appear clean, free from acute odor and showing no great buildup of wax.

If wax is apparent, the ears should be gently cleaned with cotton wool, and eardrops should be administered. Ask your vet to recommend a suitable product. Avoid the temptation to probe into the ear with cotton buds, as you may do some serious damage.

Check the ears are clean and smell fresh.

Nails

Nails should be kept short. Plenty of walking on concrete should keep them in trim, but sometimes it may be necessary to cut them. To this day, cutting a dog's nails is the one job I absolutely hate (as do my dogs) but it has to be done. I find the guillotine type of nail clippers the easiest to use.

It is imperative that you start trimming nails when your puppy is small and manageable. Just trim a sliver off the end, making sure that you avoid the quick. If you are of faint heart, leave nail-cutting to your vet.

COAT CARE

As regards grooming, all your Boxer needs is a weekly rubdown, ideally with a rubber grooming mitt. This is made of heavy-duty rubber, studded on one side. It not only gently drags out loose and dead hairs, but it also helps to massage your Boxer and tone him up. For smartness, his white trim, if he has such, can always be enhanced with the aid of a chalk block.

Sometimes, you may notice a little dry skin, causing dandruff or scurf. The cause of this is probably dietary, and a little margarine added to the food will probably clear it up. If it persists, consult your vet.

Even in the most fastidious of households, dogs can pick up fleas. The best plan is to take preventive action. Spot-on treatments have proved to be very effective, and they are very simple to apply. Ask your vet to recommend a suitable product.

Dogs that live in the countryside where livestock graze can pick up ticks. These parasites fasten themselves on to the dog's skin by a mouthpiece and suck blood. Do not pull them out, as you will probably leave the mouthpiece embedded in the dog's skin, eventually causing an

The Boxer coat is easy to care for.

abscess. To remove a tick, soak cotton wool in a mild disinfectant and apply directly to the tick for a few minutes, and the tick will then release its hold coming away intact.

Lyme disease (spread by deer ticks) is a serious disease in both dogs and humans, and is endemic to some parts of the United States and Canada. Consult your vet about vaccination or other preventive measures.

Top right: A rubber mitt is ideal for a weekly rubdown.

Right: A spot-on treatment will prevent fleas infesting the coat.

BATHTIME

There should be no need to bathe your Boxer more than twice a year if he is regularly groomed, but some Boxers have a nasty habit of rolling in all manner of unpleasant things and, in such cases, a bath is the only answer. Just as with nail-clipping and mouth-opening, my advice is to give your Boxer his first bath when he is about 16 weeks old and is small enough to restrain if he happens to freak out at his first sight of a shower nozzle. The prospect of a fully-grown male Boxer being hauled into and out of a bath for the first time ever is truly daunting.

5 TRAINING YOUR BOXER

The Boxer is a highly intelligent breed whose physical conformation, steady temperament and great brain capacity make him a versatile dog who can perform to a wide variety of tasks.

Boxers have been trained to a remarkably high level to fulfil specialist roles with the armed and police forces, they have served as guide dogs and, in competition work, they have acquitted themselves well at both Schutzhund and Championship Obedience level. Currently, Agility is a growing sport, and the Boxer's boundless energy and inherent sense of fun make him a perfect Agility dog.

As your Boxer puppy grows up, you may wish to get involved in specialized activities. To begin with, however, you will be aiming for a moderate level of obedience, which will ensure that your dog is well acquainted with the social graces and is a pleasure to live with. Training a Boxer puppy to such a standard is well within the capabilities of the average dog owner, as so much training is basic common sense.

HOUSEBREAKING

Your basic training will begin with housebreaking. Your Boxer must be taught that fouling indoors is not allowed, and he will soon become trained.

Firstly, when you get up in the morning, be sure to let your Boxer puppy out into the yard, or whatever area you have decided is acceptable as his toilet. Watch over him until he has "performed" and then make a big fuss of him.

When your puppy has finished eating a meal, put him out again, watching until he is finished, always rewarding with praise. Last thing at night, your puppy should be given the final chance of the day to relieve himself before bed.

If you get into the habit of toileting your puppy first thing in the morning, after every meal, and last thing at night, he will soon become spotlessly clean in the house.

ACCIDENTS WILL HAPPEN

Inevitably, there will be the odd accident. If the puppy produces an indoor puddle or pile in your company, and you see it happening, scold him with a loud and firm "No!" and immediately put him out into his designated toilet area. If, however, you find a mistake that the puppy has obviously left earlier, it is pointless scolding him, as he will not associate his earlier wrongdoing with your present ill temper.

CORRECTIVE TRAINING

From an early age, your puppy will, from time to time, do something that he should not. When teething, there will be the temptation to chew anything and everything. Make sure that your puppy has plenty of toys on which he can have a good gnaw. It is important that your puppy is given his own toys.

The old-fashioned idea of giving a puppy a slipper is a stupid one. If it's okay to chew an old slipper, why would it not be equally acceptable to tackle a brand-new pair of shoes? To the puppy, there will be little difference.

STICK TO THE HOUSE RULES

Your Boxer puppy will quickly realize that he is part of your family if he is properly treated. Boxers are natural "people dogs," so it follows that your puppy will want to be with you. He may well attempt to get up on the furniture and share your armchair when you are watching television. Bouncing a 10-week-old puppy on your lap may be fun, but will you be that keen on the idea when he is fully grown? Even a well-groomed Boxer will lose hair, and you may not want dog hairs on your furniture.

Therefore, it is essential from the start to establish what is acceptable, and what is not. Your Boxer should be clear in his own mind which places are out of bounds.

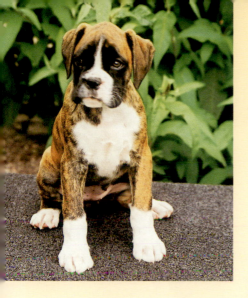

important to remain calm and never lose your temper. Boxers may appear to be tough and boisterous, but, in fact, they are quite sensitive dogs.

The Boxer is lively and intelligent, and will soon learn acceptable behavior.

Personally, I recommend a dog bed of some sort, placed near your own furniture or safely at the side of the fireplace (dogs love to get near the heat). I find the foam-walled, oval-shaped beds with detachable and washable covers are ideal for this purpose. When you are relaxing, the puppy can be placed in such a bed, with a few toys, and he will soon get the message.

When your Boxer puppy starts to chew something that is forbidden, when he tries to leap on the sofa, or contemplates any other misdemeanor, a short, loud, firm "No!", with perhaps a gentle tap on the nose, should be sufficient to convey your displeasure.

If your puppy fails to get the message, you must be more firm and exert your authority. However, it is

LEASH-TRAINING

From an early age, your Boxer puppy must be introduced to a collar and leash. I do not agree with keeping a collar on a dog all the time, as I believe it could be potentially dangerous. However, this is a matter of choice.

When you are away from home, your dog must be on the leash at all times and, if you are able to find a secure open space where he can run free, then he should always wear a collar bearing your home telephone number.

Start off with a light leather or nylon adjustable collar. Put it on your puppy when you are about to start a game. He should not be unduly worried by it and, if he is a little wary, your game will soon distract him. Each day, give your puppy a ten-minute session wearing the collar until he is totally relaxed about it.

When the pup has accepted wearing a collar, attach the leash.

Attaching a Leash

The next step is to attach a leash to the collar during your play session, just allowing it to trail behind. In this way, your Boxer will soon get used to the sense of something beyond the collar.

Once he is quite unconcerned by the leash, you can begin to hold it. To start with, simply follow your puppy around the yard, letting him take the lead. After a few sessions like this, you can introduce a little discipline.

Walk in a straight line, with your puppy at your left side. If he tugs, encourage him to come back into position, using a treat or a toy as an enticement, if necessary.

With practice, your puppy will soon get used to walking at your side and, for this exercise, the standard "Heel" command can be used. In conjunction with this routine leash-training, further commands of "Right," "Left" and "Stop" can be implemented, their use being self-explanatory.

All the basic leash-training should be done at home or in a quiet area, free from distractions. It is inadvisable to introduce your Boxer to town and traffic before he is leash-trained, the consequences could be serious.

MAKE SURE IT'S FUN

Keep training sessions short, as your puppy has a limited concentration span. Break up training exercises with a game, it is important that your pup learns that training is fun. If your pup is struggling with an exercise, go back to basics and ask him to do something easy. Then you can praise him and end the session on a good note. Remember, little and often is the key to successful training.

THE SIT

A dog that will sit on command is a pleasure to have around and will never make a nuisance of himself. Teaching a dog to sit can be done quite simply with example and reward. Boxers enjoy their food and an edible prize at the end of a successful training session will soon get the message across.

You can use a treat to lure your pup into the correct position. Simply hold the treat just above your pup's head, and as he looks up at it, he will go into the Sit. Immediately reward him with the treat and plenty of praise.

Repeat this exercise a couple of times, giving the command "Sit" as your pup goes into position and he will soon get the idea. You can also practice this exercise at

A pup will learn to sit on command in no time.

mealtimes, holding the bowl just above your puppy's head, and then giving him his food when he is sitting nicely.

THE STAY

Once your puppy has mastered the Sit, you can introduce the Stay. Start off with your puppy in the Sit, and stand facing him, just a few feet away. Repeat the "Stay" command as you gradually take a few paces back.

Your puppy should remain in the Stay for a few moments when you have come to a standstill.

Then you can give the "Come" command, or simply call his name, and he should bound towards you in anticipation of your forthcoming praise.

You can teach your pup to stay in the Sit, the Stand, or the Down, slowly building up the length of time.

Build up the Stay in easy stages.

HOW TO TEACH THE DOWN

This is a useful exercise to teach; if you are ever in an emergency situation, a quick response to the command "Down" could be a lifesaver.

Start off with your dog on the leash in the Sit, and show him that you have a treat in your hand. Lower your hand to the floor and, with any luck, your pup will follow his nose and go into the Down position. If he is a little hesitant, apply gentle pressure on his shoulders to encourage him to go into the correct position. Give the command "Down" when your pup is in position, and wait a few seconds before giving him the treat and releasing him. This exercise should be built up slowly, gradually increasing the time the pup stays in the Down.

EASY DOES IT!

The secret to successful basic training is little and often. Do not leave your puppy for four days and then attempt an hour-long session. Your Boxer will lose all sense of continuity and will get bored during the irregular training.

TRAINING CLASSES

It is well worthwhile to take your Boxer to training classes. You will benefit from having an instructor to help you overcome problems, and your Boxer will benefit from socializing with other dogs.

Check out the training club before you go along with your Boxer, and find out the following:

● Are there classes especially for puppies?

● Is the instructor familiar with the Boxer temperament?

● Are training methods reward-based?

It is important that you are happy with the way the class is run, and you feel it is an environment where you and your Boxer will feel happy and relaxed.

Many clubs now teach the Good Citizen scheme, run by

Your Boxer will benefit from working in a training class.

the national kennel clubs. There are several levels of achievement, with each demanding slightly more expertise from you and your dog.

ADVANCED TRAINING

Once you have achieved a basic level of Obedience, you may decide you would like to test your Boxer's intelligence and reach a higher standard.

Competitive Obedience

This is a discipline that requires a high degree of accuracy and control. Your Boxer must learn the following skills (at different levels):
- precision heelwork,
- stays (Sit, Stand and Down),
- recalls,
- retrieving a dumbbell (progressing to other articles),
- sendaway and directed jumps,
- scent discrimination,
- distance control.

Agility

This is a fast-moving sport that is enjoyed equally by dogs and handlers. It has become increasingly popular, and there are now many specialist clubs that specialize in training for this discipline.

Each dog must complete an obstacle, competing against the clock. Faults are incurred for not clearing an obstacle, missing the contact area where the dog must get on or off certain pieces of equipment, and for taking the wrong course.

If you keep your Boxer lean and fit, there is no reason why he should not do well in the sport.

The agile Boxer: taking the weaves and the tire at speed.

WORKING TRIALS ARE A REAL TEST

There are several events that test a dog's skills: Obedience, Tracking, Agility and Schutzhund. The exercises include:

- Heeling on and off leash,
- Recalls,
- Stays,
- Sendaway,
- Retrieving a dumbbell,
- Tracking,
- Clear jump,
- Long jump,
- Scale.

SHOW TRAINING

If your Boxer puppy matures into an excellent example of his breed, you may wish to try your hand at showing him. If you do, you should start at the lowest level with a Match or Exemption show. These are usually held in conjunction with larger general shows, or arranged specifically as fundraising events for a local charity.

In order to avoid potential embarrassment, your Boxer will need to be trained for the show ring. In beauty shows, there is no need for your Boxer to sit. He must learn how to stand in the traditional show pose, displaying the typical Boxer outline.

He must also be happy about the judge examining his mouth, handling the rest of his body, and—in the case of males—checking his testicles. From an early age your puppy must get used to strangers handling him like this.

The judge will evaluate all aspects of conformation.

SECRETS OF THE SHOW POSE

To stand or "set up" your Boxer, firstly put one hand under his neck, and the other under his brisket (the forepart of his body, between the chest and the forelegs). Gently lift the dog up into position so that his front legs are well under him, and are set parallel when looking at the dog head-on. Keeping one hand under the neck, so that his head remains proud and high, run your other hand down the back of the neck and along the back in a stroking motion. Gently lift up the hindquarters and drop them back into position so that the angulation of the stifles is noticeable, and the hocks are at 90 degrees to the ground. Your Boxer should always hold his tail high, but if he finds all this mauling about a little daunting, you can encourage him by just tickling the underside of this tail, which should have the desired effect. Hold your Boxer in this position, talking quietly and reassuringly to him all the time.

MOVING YOUR DOG

The next stage is to move your Boxer as you would in the show ring. The pace is important, and you should get your Boxer used to moving alongside you at a well-coordinated trot. This is faster than a walk, but not at such a speed that the dog easily breaks stride.

He should be taught to move at this pace in a straight line, in a triangle and in a circle. At the end of moving, your Boxer should also be taught to stand free on a loose leash, ideally with his legs reverting naturally to the same position as when you stacked him.

It takes practice to move your dog correctly.

TRICKS OF THE TRADE

A Boxer will always be seen at his best when standing at the end of a loose leash, with his attention captured by something intriguing in the distance. Boxer exhibitors are notorious for throwing "attention-getters" in the ring, these varying from chunks of garlic-flavored baked liver to fur toys, along with the ubiquitous squeaky ball. Take my advice and do not attempt to "throw." It is not necessary if your Boxer is well schooled.

DOG DISTRACTIONS

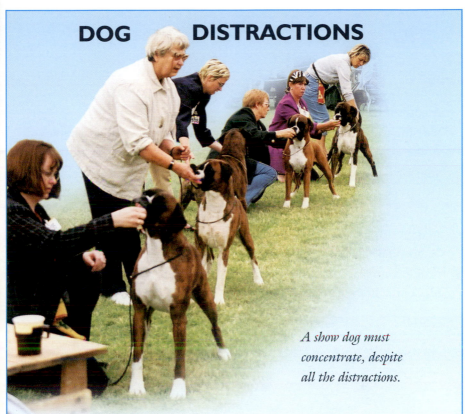

A show dog must concentrate, despite all the distractions.

When a pet Boxer goes into a show ring environment for the first time, a major problem that is often experienced is that the dog is not used to standing nose-to-tail with other dogs; despite your religious training efforts, his concentration wanders to the new-found chums on either side of him. This can be helped by getting friends to bring their dogs to your home for mock show sessions. However, it is far better to attend a ringcraft (ring training) class where experienced handlers will give you excellent advice and school your dog in what is essentially an authentic show environment.

TRAINING FOR THE COMMUNITY

You have now trained your young Boxer to be a model of decorum; he is obedient and a pleasure to be with.

There may be many people in your own community who would love to be able to share their life with a dog but, through no fault of their own, cannot. These may be hospitalized children, young people with learning difficulties at residential homes, or the elderly who may have been forced to give up their homes, and possibly their pets.

There are several charitable organizations such as St. John's Therapy Dogs, that are always happy to accept new dogs and owners on their books so that they may become part of a visiting program. Prior to acceptance, your Boxer will be tested for character and

A well-trained Boxer (or two) is a pleasure to own.

temperament. If you do become involved in one of these programs, you will derive enormous satisfaction from seeing how much pleasure your very own Boxer can bring to the less fortunate. It can be a most rewarding exercise.

Breed Ambassador

You should always remember that you are privileged to be a Boxer owner: you have a responsibility to maintain the breed's reputation. Your Boxer should be a great advertisement for the breed, with sound temperament and impeccable manners.

With correct training, your Boxer should bring joy to everyone he meets and act as an ambassador *par excellence*. The breed has a noble heritage of which you should be proud.

You owe it to your dog, and the breed, to ensure that he preserves the good name of the Boxer breed.

Nothing beats the fun of being with a Boxer.

6 HEALTH CARE

The Boxer is a naturally hardy breed and relatively maintenance-free. However, each week, when you are giving him his regular grooming session, you should check his ears, eyes, teeth and coat.

If your Boxer appears to be off-color or off his food, give him 24 hours and, if there is no noticeable improvement, contact your vet. Symptoms spotted early can often prevent a condition becoming more serious.

COMMON AILMENTS

Anal Glands

You need to look out for problems with the anal glands. These are two glands situated at either side of the anus. Sometimes, and for no apparent reason, they can become impacted. The indication of this happening could be your Boxer dragging himself along on his rear end, a barely apparent swelling in this area, or the occasional detection of a foul smell. Expressing the glands is simple, taking just seconds, an experienced hand and a good supply of tissues, but it is best left to the vet.

Inexperienced attempts could cause mild injury.

Bloat

Bloat is a condition that results from fermenting foods releasing gas into the stomach, sometimes causing the stomach to twist. It is a serious condition, and it must be dealt with instantly by your vet as it can prove fatal. There are various theories as to the cause of bloat, but none are scientifically proven.

As a preventive, it is advisable to feed two small meals rather than one large meal if a complete diet is used, and exercise should not happen until a few hours after a meal.

Burns

Burns and scalds should be dealt with immediately. Apply cold water to the affected area to ease the pain, then take your dog to the vet as soon as possible.

Never exercise your Boxer immediately after feeding.

Cuts and wounds

Inevitably, at some stage of your Boxer's life, he will suffer a minor cut or a wound of some sort. In the case of small cuts and gashes, cleaning with a mild disinfectant and treating with an antiseptic ointment should be all that is necessary. Larger wounds may need stitching by your veterinarian, and deep wounds may be subject to infection, requiring a course of antibiotics.

Cut pads can be difficult to deal with, for obvious reasons. However, if the cut is small, cleaning as detailed above can soon be followed by treating with a proprietary brand of "new skin" solution, which is painted on and forms a protective layer, thus speeding the healing process.

Cysts

Boxers are prone to developing small cysts in middle age and beyond. Most remain small and benign, and may never require treatment. However, if a cyst seems to be growing rapidly, veterinary advice should be sought. Interdigital cysts (between the toes) can often be painful, and these may require surgery.

Heatstroke

Most Boxers love the sun, but too

It is all too easy for the Boxer to get overheated.

Beware: the inquisitive Boxer may land himself in trouble.

much sunbathing can bring on heatstroke. If your Boxer is adversely affected, he will be shaky on his legs and his temperature will be unduly high. Try to reduce the temperature by applying ice packs (large packs of frozen peas from your freezer, wrapped in a towel, are ideal in an emergency), and keep the dog in a cool, shady place.

Never leave your Boxer in a car, even on a moderately warm day, as a parked car will serve as an oven. Dogs die in hot cars regularly, so make sure you never take the risk.

Poisoning

Boxers are curious, and your dog may be tempted to chew at something in your yard that may present a potential danger. If you notice that your Boxer is a little shaky on his legs, glassy-eyed, and rather disoriented, there is a chance that he has taken in a noxious substance.

You should contact your vet immediately, with details of what you suspect may have been ingested (if you know). Of course, you should always keep chemicals out of your Boxer's reach.

Stings

Boxers are fascinated by bees, wasps, and other buzzing insects. Often, their curiosity is harmless, but occasionally, a sting will result. If this is external, treat the area with an antiseptic solution, and then apply a paste of baking soda and water. If the sting is in the mouth, apply ice cubes to the affected area and consult your vet immediately.

Stomach Upsets

Routinely, you should get into the habit of checking your Boxer's motions when you clean up after him.

They should always be firm and free from worms. If they are loose, your Boxer probably has an upset stomach. The best course of action is to starve your dog for 24 hours, making sure that fresh drinking water is readily available. When you resume feeding, offer plain food, such as fish or cooked chicken and rice. If your Boxer still has diarrhea, consult your vet without any further delay.

In the case of a stomach upset, restrict food for 24 hours.

Kennel Cough

This condition is highly infectious so, at the first sign of coughing, isolate your dog and consult the vet. If you take your dog to the vet's office, do not go into the waiting room; ask to go straight into the consulting room. The vet may prefer to examine your dog in the car.

Kennel cough usually occurs where there are large gatherings of other dogs, such as in boarding kennels or at dog shows. The first sign of the disease is when a dog coughs after exercise or when he is excited. Owners often mistake this for the dog having something stuck in his throat.

Treatment is usually a course of antibiotics; keeping your dog warm, quiet and dry will aid recovery. There are vaccinations available for kennel cough, and most boarding kennels will insist that your dog is vaccinated.

Sarcoptic Mange

This can affect a dog at any age, although it is more common in puppies. A parasitic mite lives in the skin and causes irritation to the dog. This, in turn, causes the dog to scratch, which inflames the skin and leads to hair loss. The areas most commonly affected are the muzzle, the ears, the stomach and the legs.

The vet may take a skin scraping for examination. Parasitic washes are usually prescribed to kill off the mites. Remember that sarcoptic mange is highly infectious, so you must isolate an infected dog.

Demodectic Mange

This is not as common as sarcoptic mange, and is usually seen in puppies up to nine months old. The mite lives in the hair follicles, and bald patches start to appear on the face, chest and legs. Treatment is with parasitic washes and antibiotics. This type of mange is not infectious to other dogs.

Cystitis

Cystitis is where the bladder becomes inflamed. The first symptoms are frequent passing of urine, and discomfort when doing so. You should consult your vet for a suitable treatment. It will help if you take a small sample of urine with you. To do this, place a flat dish under the dog, then transfer the urine to a bottle.

MANGE

There are two types of mange: sarcoptic and demodectic.

INHERITED CONDITIONS

Progressive Axonopathy (PA)

In the U.K. in the late 1970s, several Boxer breeders reported cases of Boxer puppies, sometimes as old as 6 months, going off their back legs and gradually becoming paralyzed. The condition turned out to be Progressive Axonopathy, a debilitating disease that affects the nervous system, is incurable, and is hereditary.

It was determined that the PA gene was a simple recessive and, to this day, there is no certainty as to how or why it should appear. In practical terms, this meant that two healthy carriers could be bred and produce puppies that were affected by PA.

Despite initial turmoil within the breed, Boxer breeders and the Boxer Breed Council rallied together and implemented measures to eradicate the disease. Top-winning dogs were castrated and given away to pet homes, hitherto valuable brood bitches were spayed, and some breeders had simply to start from scratch with newly-acquired breeding stock (a lot of which was imported

Major checks are now carried out on all breeding stock.

from other countries where PA was unheard of). PA cases are now rarely seen, but the U.K. breeders are very vigilant in monitoring for signs.

Degenerative Myelopathy (DM)

This is a potentially debilitating neurological condition that can eventually paralyze its victims, and occurs with relative frequency in Boxers. The cause of DM remains unknown and it is particularly frustrating because the signs of the condition—progressive spinal weakness and paralysis—do not usually appear until later in life, after a dog has been used in a breeding program.

Because there is no screening test, DM is considered a "rule-out" condition in which other mimicking conditions, such as a disc condition or tumors, must be eliminated, leaving DM as the conclusion. At present, a definitive identification of DM can only be determined post-mortem.

Signs usually appear when a dog is between 5 and 9 years old. It begins with a loss of coordination in the hind legs, and the dog may wobble or drag its feet. The condition generally progresses from rear leg paralysis to foreleg paralysis to respiratory failure within the span of a year. No pain appears to be associated with the paralysis, but of course there is the discomfort of the dog being unable to continue his active lifestyle, and the pain of the owner watching this happen.

HEART CONDITIONS

Some Boxer lines seem to be affected with heart problems. This may mean nothing more than a slight murmur that will not affect a Boxer's quality of life at all; others may be more serious.

If you are planning to breed from your Boxer bitch, you should do your utmost to ensure that she is physically fit enough for the whelping, and heart testing should be considered essential. Testing sessions are arranged at many Boxer shows, but your vet can also carry out the simple test.

If you plan to breed from your bitch, it is wise to carry out a heart test.

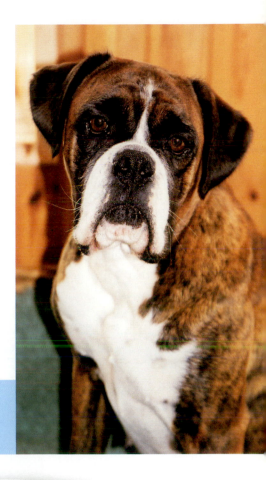

HIP DYSPLASIA (HD)

HD is another hereditary condition that affects some Boxers to a minor degree. Ascertaining the level of dysplasia, if it exists, involves x-raying a dog under general anaesthetic, and the resulting x-rays are then sent to a professional body, which scores them.

THE VETERAN BOXER

As your Boxer enters the last few years of life, he will find difficulty in doing much of what was taken for granted when in his prime. He will generally take things more slowly, and some of his vital organs may let him down.

Old dogs, like old people, become arthritic. It is, therefore, essential that your ageing Boxer has a bed that is firm yet soft, low to the ground, and completely draft-free. There are several types of bed available that are manufactured especially for the elderly dog. Exercise should be reduced if your dog has become arthritic.

As time goes by, your Boxer may require medication to help with a condition that has developed with old age. In this

There will come a time when your Boxer starts to slow down.

The elderly Boxer can still enjoy a good quality of life.

case, veterinary advice should always be followed. Your Boxer's meals can be reduced slightly in quantity, but increase the frequency of meals. A high consumption of fluids may signal the onset of ailing kidneys.

Caring for the veteran Boxer requires patience and understanding; at all times, the quality of life should be uppermost in your mind. A change of lifestyle may be called for but, with minor adjustments, many Boxers enjoy their golden years.

THE FINAL PARTING

Much as it pains us, dogs do not live nearly as long as we would like them to. Boxers, on average, live for around 12 years or so.

It is every dog owner's hope that their pal will, when the time has come, die peacefully in his sleep, thus relieving his owner of the terrible burden of having to make a heartrending decision.

Quality Question

Should your Boxer become old and infirm, what should be uppermost in your mind is his quality of life. Too many owners put off making "that" decision, not out of concern for the dog, but to spare their own feelings, which is wrong. Your Boxer will have led a happy, active life. If he becomes incontinent, or crippled with arthritis, he will lose his pride and his independence.

You will know when the time has come to part.

When this happens, you must think long and hard if it is really the kindest thing to drag out a life that is becoming miserable.

Life Cycle

Your Boxer will have given you 100 percent loyalty throughout his life. You owe it to him to do the same, and there may come a time when the kindest thing for your Boxer is to ensure that he leaves this world with dignity.

His passing will leave a great void in your life, and you may feel you can never give your heart to another Boxer.

But time heals, and you will gradually remember all the good times you spent together, all the joy he brought you, and the thrill you felt when you first saw the face of that mischievous little puppy.

And that is when it all starts again.

The best compliment is to start again with a new puppy.

ABOUT THE AUTHOR

Andrew Brace is one of the U.K.'s leading all-around judges, approved to award Kennel Club Challenge Certificates in some 50 breeds. In addition, he has been approved to judge Best in Show at Championship level, as well as the Working, Utility, Toy and Hound Groups.

For many years, Andrew has written a weekly column in the British paper *Dog World*, as well as making monthly contributions to the U.S.'s *Dog News*, Australia's *Ozdog*, and *Dogs in Canada*. As a breeder and exhibitor, Andrew is best known for his Beagles, the most famous to carry his Tragband affix being Ch. Too Darn Hot For Tragband, who remains the top-winning Beagle of all time in the U.K.